Umwelt

Dorothy Lehane

Open House Editions

Published by Open House Editions, an imprint of Leafe Press

www.leafepress.com

ISBN: 978-0-9574048-6-1

Cover artwork "From Both Sides Now" © Emmy Verschoor.
Used with kind permission of the artist.

Acknowledgements

With thanks to the editors of the following journals and websites; Cordite Poetry Review, Snow 3, Shearsman, Tears in the Fence, Molly Bloom, Long Poem Magazine, datableed and Litmus: the haematological issue.

With special thanks to Emmy Verschoor for the cover artwork.

Thanks to Kat Peddie and Ben Hickman for reading early versions of this work. Thanks to Elinor Cleghorn and Sarah Crewe for all your love and support, and to Mark, for teaching me how to survive.

Umwelt

and truth rampages / across all this demanding honesty

David Chaloner

Visiting the hands & lips, =

Feel so tongue in mouth

so tongue in throat

so tongue in heart

so embodied tongue

so tongue in rouge

so rouge in ruin

tongue in bond

Re-trigger the uncovering of voice

non-voice, for "credible testimony"

In extremis: I moved very close to you

closer to death to the death of the world

Litany for an absent personhood

Informed consent: you moved away

& here I am keeping us in it

At times I called out MONSTER

We never talk body fluids

The couch & my vicarious trauma

"Informed" breach

Release form   dialogue multiplies

Unmediated, my worries about the real world

The implications of my witness

"I am talking to you, but there is always your audience to consider"

: F— you, phallogocentric world

My body, full of his grief words

this impasse which began

in authorial conflict: my body ingesting grief

/in my vignettes, always grieving

—I am something, but it is not—

Writing in the dark, dropping out important-ataxic-words

Your apparatus is complete in the way

verbal machinery is annexed while the body still roams

Forgive me for taking your name

& disfiguring you/ forgive

how each world ends when the body is a throne of abuse

the woman & my interdependence & my soliloquy

tell me you will live —tell the voices

but the bronchi, just about locale

tell the bronchi this year ends in Lautbilder

The camera was a gun I couldn't point. (Cherry Smyth)

This is the long lesson of straying from image

Tell the bronchi the flames are imagined

Unspoiled moments smooth out into

the wellspring is here but I am

not drinking

culture in my saliva

apropos an un-writing

to account for a spine

velar plosive   hard as in gravel

gargoyle, soft as in gesture, ginger

social pleasures during our third winter

social pleasures rely on the pineal gland

both alert & mute   I didn't steal your tongue

if the tongue is shared the apple is shared

you   are   no   more   perverse

in your musculature

no more social pleasures except how the concept of self-unravels

when you are phonic

We will never define dis-fluency as screaming at the roaring sea

we will define dis-fluency by asking where have all the images gone

Whisper or pantomime speech

fluency returns when we whisper or pantomime speech

The route between bone & air

sure my jaw & mouth are apparatus & need more attention

to create the perfect side-tone

Of course, /they do not notice, occupied in the whirling/ reinvigoration of

themselves. (How could they notice?) – Rilke (trans. Martyn Crucefix)

During the block you aren't sure if it is abnormal high tension

or the language centres but the time taken to speak a passage

becomes indicative of another passage

& we are reminded that

you tend to be wandering in the night

reforming yourself into pauses & prolongations

I am far from fluent in the morning

far from thinking faster than I can talk

Mothers in shock   low ebb

well what happened to the mother

mother on a careless ebb

You are becoming well

but I have started napping in the day

shutting myself off   minimizing

The body forms a peninsular

connected to others but soft & drowned

I think it over   seems a discrepancy or expression of remembrance

Everyday the sea revives, you never hear of it wilting

Everyday the sea revives, you never hear of it wilting

Everyday the sea revives, you never hear of it wilting

The poem as a target for pathology

Heritable & Leave me

be home before Christmas

The d-dimer is positive

This acute present

Grows in the faking orgasms

The body abates

allows some fucking time We are fucking

in a different way to before I can't help think of

the stations of the cross Each new position

— the antebellum body— You won't find

a more screwed up & sagacious example of settlement

Collapse with me, I really wish you would collapse

Give me your hand, your meta-ill struggle

Celebrate the new embodiment

& the faking of the acute present

this hot new need

for a pillow for each affected joint

Nothing outside the window if you are asking

Other limbs // oddities are unruly

Why is my oath living outside your oath?

The surgeon takes a call to his son

Speaking half Greek half English

the patient has been reading

We care so much about poetry we consider this disease an intervention

The permanent marks

are to do with moments I will return to you

I prefer it like this Gagging with the idea

of the body Striving to do violence

to the things we must accept

Transience in the industry

I am okay ever other 20 hours or so

not sure if we talk too much

or not enough

swelling iambs

to see you coming into the room

do not allow the tongue to riot

we have seen what can be effaced

plus   the difficulty with swallowing

The throaty oesophageal tissue dislodges

as if to say here be nourishment & battle

Keep going & Peer at the womb that haemorrhages post-coitally

Remove the tube & it's still a sticky mess

So fraught & such Arcadia

Didn't you hear enough of the brutality

Erode your name it doesn't lift me

He outlaw'd coffee

Tore the stitches out

with his tongue

Part-time venom

surges at the brunt of attack

Unthinkable: the way you held me in your contract

These days we don't even take our clothes off

A million practices beholden Textures of disobedience

& textures of entry I am thinking of a hiatal place:

a rupture Remember child: he's just a boy

Just a human boy He fills up and empties out same as all of us

we favour disfluency

how human-abstract this study is

in the soundboard of profundo—

the void in widow

the void in mother

some lesions run deeper

than can be screened for

in the right hemisphere

witness this super arrangement

sound blurring into auditory & pictorial

a final shaping flowing backwards

from the alveolar ridge

what excites my cortex is often

exposure—

you hang up another jargon

neologisms oscillating

between spectator

& verisimilitude

there's no being closer to me

than helping my wayward angular gyrus

recall repartee   :   girlhood versus

the corpus of dull

& in its abeyance

far more than muted tension

// stress signal

enduring the minus hours

past the furore of outpouring

happy in your orgy

—your scansion ((girl in wellspring))

so much to let in

reading long before light

your craft   we go as far as

total-body total-plexus

it's neoclassic   multifocal episodes

unfolding at the dinner table

verbs in abeyance

bypass error

the skill of circumlocution

after much labour

after much correction

lest we forget

your pre-morbid brilliance

— whiling away time with

Greek epigrams—

the detriment goes deeper

at night the words fall

indigestible & erudite

this solo is a rest

metabolically vital

my my   so many ways

to croon over erosion

federal census says mammae are painful

& full   mammae is the state of the ovaria

mammae be crying   & full of epinephrine

female malady gutsy fits gutsy multi-vocal fits

federal census says plexus no longer confined

to the body   the body

does its own talking   love-sick swearing

federal census says stimulate her peculiar delicacy

stimulate the embedded trunk of nerves   give her

a lancet for those spasms   &   suppress her mammea

mammea be full of gossip   mammea be tense &

offensive   curating hype for libido   curating viscous

animal exit   federal census says try routes of

physical testament   soothe here says the census

do not employ the lancet   &   do not be desired

federal census says rampancy so soon

after conception   rampancy as reversible hosiery

each month be rampancy & moral sensibility

female ovaria   &   the noise of moral sadness

suffering rubbishing rubbishing

Your jaw is goals Your dentist

wants clitoris Is ready with her lance attack & scalpel –

YR an elaborate childhood moment

Concern not just for self but also regarding duty & trouble carrying it

Held in moment of exquisite rebellion Sure-sure

subside & go-go & gradually creep out Make a new place

it's Le pivot goals Let pivot orgasm

the last, inevitable surface you won't go out tonight

for this faded conman Get paler Be among

the gene-pool is to be stuffed by taxidermy

Assemble yrs of complaint A mix of negligence

& fuck you & dope dope & IVdrips & IVdrips

until you are wrecked in the face & delusional

Why nurses nurse the SUCK in bathroom

He hoodwinks You evidence Witness impasse

But that's the way people are

Derive // or drift // detourning that

moniker // amped up drool

just past Wheeler St.

Overlooking   if u have the ear for it

lip-sync //my film stills

triste tristtd try try bunny games   :

bunnybunnybunnybunnyquerulantwhooops

cataracts for regeneration

persecutory lawsuits: air spittin

I'm keen keen keen

hi FATHER OF MY FATHER OF MY FATHER

don't don't lip sync

can I sex your leg can I

breach yr hand does your hand

still manage

can you still hold a dick

Do not approve

At midnight but because it wraps itself

by jove

i want any slight dampness that is present

Fiddling, this is dishonest

(I am not a sexy fireman & it is disrespectful

to all real sexy

fireman to pretend I am)

Can't get off on

just looking at my actual body

by the globule   & migrating across the face

Count the marriage lines

Too polite for the Semester to end this way

This devastating MAN AT YOUR KNEES humour

Rouse suspicions with a round of bellicose

Whoever left love unscarred never left

Redressing the bodies of the dead

fevers derived from the architecture of moods

Marshal in remission lasting between one day & six months

This pilfering & endlessly astray body

Every arrangement is happening

except serological work: the

gamma globulin series

occupying lung space

STOP writing about wombs you sick fuck

We know you've got to live & the Eulogists

will look for signs that just one more assault is good for the elegy

I'm here for the home stretch This patch of

Mottlement   enjambed internally

We have to be quick   & sequential

So you are faced with dying & nobody is intervening

ask if cognitive dysfunction is part of it

It requires something to remain coping &

often I mother the children in a way that implies

I've just found them under my care

Undifferentiated Absence is within us

Multisensory the spectrum we use for the invulnerability of love

Put the burn on me you don't need to attack me

Vulgar lover the would-be long night Lolling head & mouth &

No seam between To feel a surge of pride

Are we boycotting countries or just too poor to travel

Deforested & corroded : here in these spaces

new password new password

hello Dorothy 25% off winter

& my heart is a layaway

Off to Parson's green

for an amuse bouche or two

Rewards for the latest bloods

There's a new ecosystem growing

Just you wait until your funeral

& we laugh: sure of the refusal

Shut-up & consider hieroglyphs

& wait in case the antidote is digitalised

I didn't think the girl could be so cruel:

there's an almost hospital level sanitary nature to her

TESTING Clinical Mothers

testing is psycho-dynamic

loss of thoracic breathing

& with heavy trunk attack

483 records of stuttering

seeking vocalization

of inferior endocrine environments

or the crowded number 39

Cold-Harborough Lane

in the offspring of the skilled

& unskilled under observation

120 clinical mothers crooning

ba-ba-baby

30 of these 66 mothers

do not rate hypertonic severity

avoidance in the subgroups

co-existing and holding good

these are real problems— really existing—

group 5 problems

in addition to organic psychoses

paralysis of musculature speech

& not receiving reliable sensory information

there's never relearning the route round the house

we are surviving one type of death

a heedless sort of narcissist death

thoughts are unitary

sentient in that moment

grant me license to dismantle all previous experience

under the trope of consummation

the linguist   made up of the radical

is post-operatively mainlining stimulus

explains proverbs

the jaw deviates to the right on excursion

the patient chokes

the patient can initiate phonation for 5 seconds

can protract and retract tongue

neglect items on the right

in the absence of the volta

you precious, cool motherfucker

95th percentile the way that sonnet begins

'thoracic' is a very ugly word for better or worse

you & your nervous metabolism

draw a schema of your normcore thrill

in the beginning was neurology

but then we've put mind particles away for 2015

Franz Joseph Gall and the doctrine of the skull

we've got eyes on your sense of pride

eyes on the joker/ we've got eyes

on the elevations and depressions of the skull

two year decree, growing hair like your father

nothing occurs without the agreement of d.n.a.

without the expiration of intrinsic polar separation

you might as well begin your operette morali

The cells have been carrying on without the gown knowing

& now the pattern swoops in Tiny companioned antibodies

Lulls in what is otherwise counter-diagnosis of "rheum"

& streaming tissues Disorders & disquiet

Rolls own cigarettes Antibodies swoop in:

lulls in what is otherwise counter secretion & tissue diagnosis

Antibody raids on small dreams

The over-examined body is free & salted

secreted & behandled

The gown is global, spectatorial & located

Shifting bodies Bodies at the helm of seams

The shock comes from wearing the gown

Paisley fleur-de-lis The draft beneath:

a distinct possibility of the boundaries unravelling

The shock of waiting room surveillance

Surveying & itching scales of immobilization

Baudelaire & brutality Baudelaire & perversion

Every time the blood machine beeps imagine counter violence

Embodiment is the passage between the waiting & the phlebotomist

All my versions of cure & self are rebuilt in the sublimation of authority—

take the cuts, the incisions offered but the wounds

aren't clinical The contingency is to smile

at their talk of weapons, remain hyper-present

Blood is quarantined & desperately calls out

to measure the value of body

Trespass you are trespassing

Your vinyl gloves & your sanitary codes of conduct

The self is redressed

defective until the next gaze or summons

I am finished with beauty & money Close the gap

between us which is imaginary but nonetheless

The scars within him are much more frightening

than the scars on his body There's a hint of superiority

Being Alive Staying Alive Strangled into Being

If we break-down the ethics of listening

Loving you until there is no cartilage left

Can't quite look at men my own age yet

w/ their cumbersome flirting

Call out to complexities of entanglement

What has happened to you is everywhere on the lips of strangers

tiresomely

& I'm never sure if they are talking about my faith or my body

But at least the body can count metrics & clean up its act

Who knows where we might turn in negation

The war has something to do with this entourage of medics

who are past caring

Put this in your mouth Use this for your impulse

Put this slantwise

Sung— You are so sung— The idea of future singing is lilted

& the cold   & the cold cold

done done unto body   reckless body

Remade in the vision of

Vanishing. We know not to ice it

the warmth glides by// the new year is starting

& the midwife who yanked me from one space

into another could only take me so far

The dead girls in this village   concealed scandals

living on   in their mothers' slow walks

It persists   critical awareness & anatomising

: the same deal.   & litany & cold litany

all the worthlessness   & kindling wood

we can't keep warm   & we can't dispense with silence

jettison inquiry   your loaded personalities

mothers call this burden   exoskeleton

never alone   never that cruel soft tissue

We need agency & freedom & eroticism

Here I am relentlessly in love with the reader

lapscape & common talk about the artificial

pulsing of swoon   swoon   swoon

Those who fish in the sea are free in the society

of men— dans leur ordre naturel—

I'm not putting my son   in the society of men

Their uneven way of going on   the guilt

we feel when they only have themselves to fuck

In the rumours In the politic

In the humping your leg politic

Did the boy learn from his father   his thrall

Did the boy learn from the screen

from rank or event

The byelaws give rise to implied consent

Just come   & discuss the nature of

your cellular rights   Scour & improve

your bedside manner   This breach

on the chained off good nature Write onto

my body their soundscapes No access

Just another incoherent & anaesthetising force

Defined by hospital & house bound expression

Make love to the literati   You deserve it

after this period   of anti-climax & the broad

spectrum-antibiotic   & this cytotoxic plasticity